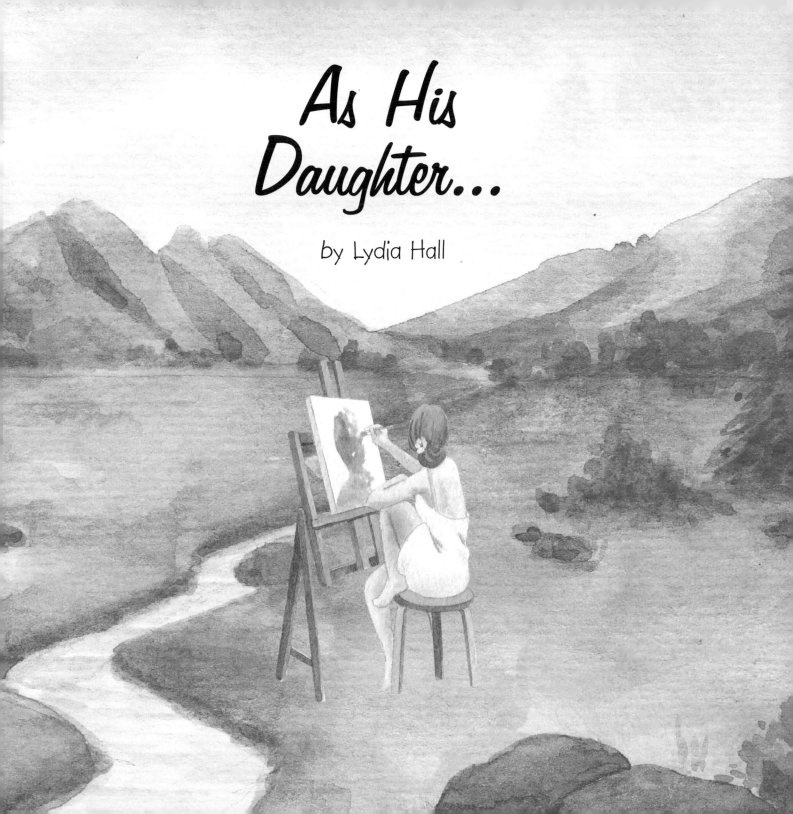

As His Daughter...

by Lydia Hall

WestBow Press books may be ordered through booksellers or by contacting:

WestBow Press
A Division of Thomas Nelson & Zondervan
1663 Liberty Drive
Bloomington, IN 47403
www.westbowpress.com
844-714-3454

ISBN: 979-8-3850-1700-3 (sc)
ISBN: 979-8-3850-1702-7 (hc)
ISBN: 979-8-3850-1701-0 (e)

Library of Congress Control Number: 2024900762

Print information available on the last page.

WestBow Press rev. date: 2/16/2024

WESTBOW
PRESS®
A DIVISION OF THOMAS NELSON
& ZONDERVAN

Dedicated to:

Everleigh Rose & Alyssa Wren!

Abide in His love,

sweet girls!

As His Daughter...

I pray this book will
help cultivate strong
Christian girls!

Let this book be a place where
you and your little one can find
confidence in the love, provision,
and promises of God the Father!

As you read these truths over
your baby girl, start each page
with "As His daughter..."
and watch together as
the scene comes alive!

The following prayers are written for:

_____

Handwritten with love by:

_____

_____

Time frame when written:

_____

Date given:

_____

As His Daughter...

Your prayer for her:

_____

_____

_____

_____

_____

_____

_____

_____

_____

_____

_____

_____

_____

_____

_____

As His Daughter...

Your prayer for her:

_____

_____

_____

_____

_____

_____

_____

_____

_____

_____

_____

_____

_____

_____

As His Daughter...

Your prayer for her:

_____
_____
_____
_____
_____
_____
_____
_____
_____
_____
_____
_____
_____
_____
_____
_____

As His
Daughter...

Your prayer for her:

_____

_____

_____

_____

_____

_____

_____

_____

_____

_____

_____

_____

_____

_____

_____

As His Daughter...

Your prayer for her:

_____
_____
_____
_____
_____
_____
_____
_____
_____
_____
_____
_____
_____
_____
_____

As His Daughter...

Your prayer for her:

_____

_____

_____

_____

_____

_____

_____

_____

_____

_____

_____

_____

_____

_____

_____

As His Daughter...

Your prayer for her:

_____

_____

_____

_____

_____

_____

_____

_____

_____

_____

_____

_____

_____

_____

_____

As His Daughter...

Your prayer for her:

_____

_____

_____

_____

_____

_____

_____

_____

_____

_____

_____

_____

_____

_____

_____

_____

As His Daughter...

Your prayer for her:

_____
_____
_____
_____
_____
_____
_____
_____
_____
_____
_____
_____
_____
_____
_____
_____

As His Daughter...

Your prayer for her:

_____
_____
_____
_____
_____
_____
_____
_____
_____
_____
_____
_____
_____
_____
_____

Printed in the United States
by Baker & Taylor Publisher Services